# The Auto Girl's Ultimate Car Care Guide

## 10 Ways to Save Tons of Money on Auto Repair

Deborah J Glazer-Wright

Copyright © 2018

Disclaimer: Deborah J Glazer-Wright presents the entire content of this program for educational purposes only. The information provided by Wright is not intended to diagnose or make recommendations on the issues you may be having on your vehicle.

All examples in this book are just that—examples. They are not intended to represent or guarantee that every car has the same symptoms, issues or be serviced in the same manner.

You understand that the maintenance for each vehicle you drive will be slightly different from the sample maintenance schedules discussed within this book. All vehicle fluid and services should be based on the manufacturer's recommendation for your specific vehicle.

Check with your local dealership or auto repair shop before performing any maintenance or repairs on your car.

# Where to find the Auto Girl:

**Blog:**
http://www.theAutoGirl.com

**Facebook**:
https://www.facebook.com/TheAutoGirl/

**Facebook Group:**
https://business.facebook.com/TheAutoGirl/

**Instagram:**
https://www.instagram.com/the_auto_girl/

**Twitter:**
https://twitter.com/theautogirl

**Pinterest:**
https://www.pinterest.com/TheAutoGirl/

**LinkedIn:**
https://www.linkedin.com/in/deborahgwright/

**YouTube:** Coming Soon!

# Dedication

This book is dedicated to my children: Tyler, Myles, Hilary, Dylan and Baylee—the loves of my life! These amazing kids of mine have encouraged me as much as I have encouraged them. Watching my kids reach their goals has been so rewarding.

They, in turn, have inspired me to do the same. I am so proud of the adults they've become. Even as they graduate from college and start into their chosen careers, they continue to call me when they have car trouble. At least now it's before they break down.

To my mom Gloria Glazer and my sister Stephanie Glazer who have been so supportive while I worked so hard to build my business. I could not have raised such amazing kids without their love, help and support.

To Joe, for always supporting me and my crazy, challenging ideas and for helping me reach my big dreams. You've helped me envision, rehearse, plan, shop, prepare, create and edit. You allowed me to dream big and supported me along the way, even when you weren't sure about where I wanted to go.

To my friends, employees and customers for their loyalty, even when it meant making the drive across town to support me and my business.

I am so thankful to everyone who has supported me emotionally, creatively and productively. I am where I am because of my community.

# Endorsements and Accolades

*"I admire Deborah Glazer-Wright for all she has accomplished in life and for succeeding in a field dominated by men. Her desire to inspire and help women take care of their vehicles provides a feeling of relief and peace of mind. She shares valuable information and tools which familiarize women and help them be proactive regarding their vehicle's maintenance to avoid unnecessary spending in repairs. Thank you, Deborah, for your help and the education you provide to so many women."*

Dr. Michelle Almeida, Clinical Psychologist, Educator, Speaker, and #1 Best Selling Author of SuperWoman in Charge: How to Protect your Sanity and Succeed in Life

# Who Should Read This Book?

## This book is for those of you who:

- Don't know what to do when it comes to car maintenance and repairs.

- Put off car repairs because you just don't want to deal with the process.

- Don't like taking your car in for service.

- Feel intimidated when talking to the service advisor.

- Want to understand the basics of your car.

- Want to learn how to save money on car repairs.

- Need to understand some basics so you can explain to your kids.

- Don't want to get stuck on the side of the road.

- Don't know enough about car repair and want to know more.

# Why Would I Buy an Auto Repair Shop?

This is the number one question that people ask me when they find out that I own an auto repair shop.

Here's my story.

My youngest was heading off to college, and I would soon be home alone. It was time for me to find something to do that would pay the bills.

While raising my kids, I hopped from job to job. These jobs offered no future or opportunity for growth - certainly not career material. The male owners were tough on me as their only employee. One employer even ripped the phone out of my hands to ask how I had placed a delivery order. When the voice on the other end confirmed I had placed the order correctly, he handed the phone back to me without an apology.

I was going nowhere fast. Eventually, I landed a job at an auto repair shop. This was finally a fun job for me. Customers became friends. I knew that just like food and makeup, customers would need to keep their cars on the road. We all count on our cars, don't we?

It was while working at this shop that I formulated my plan. I decided I should buy my own auto repair shop. Crazy, huh?

While researching the auto repair industry, I found that women were a very under served group of customers, even though women make up half of car care service buyers. At the time, I was unaware of any other women in the auto repair industry.

As a single mom, my kids have had car trouble many times. Our cars were often old and in need of repair.

I never paid attention to the fact that oil changes should be performed every 5,000 miles. I had no idea how to care for and maintain my car, much less the cars that my kids were driving.

When I took ownership of my shop, I made it my mission to educate my customers about taking care of their cars. I wanted to help them save money. I couldn't believe the number of stories I heard from women feeling they had been sold repairs they didn't need. Many felt taken advantage of (even if they needed the repairs).

When it comes to their car, many people just don't know what they need to know. As adults, we should know the basics of car care, and pass this knowledge on to our teen drivers.

Getting stuck on the side of the road can be a scary experience.

It is often costly, in terms of time away from work, a tow bill to get the car to a repair shop, and repair costs themselves.

A car is usually the second largest purchase a person makes, second to buying a home. Because a car is such a big expense, I wondered why so many drivers didn't know enough about what it takes to keep their cars safely on the road.

Think about it. You depend on your car for work and play. Doesn't it make sense to take care of your car so it will take care of you?

This book will teach you the basics and educate you on how to be prepared.

If I can teach my five kids, their significant others and their friends to take care of their cars, I can teach you too!

This book is meant to be a resource. Read it first, take notes and keep it in your glove box.

Do what it takes to be knowledgeable and prepared.

Take care of your car and it will take care of you!

*Deborah Glazer-Wright*

x

# Table of Contents

# Chapter One
## You and Your Car

*A strong woman looks a challenge dead in the eye and gives it a wink.*
*~ Gina Carey*

Owning a car gives us freedom. We depend on our car to get us around town or across the country. However, car ownership is an ongoing expense, and while it's an asset, it's a depreciating asset (it will lose value over time).

If you choose to ignore basic car care needs, your car will lose value even faster.

By properly maintaining your car, you'll slow its depreciation and enjoy a reliable ride for many years.

Car maintenance costs increase with mileage, due to wear, environmental factors, driving conditions and your driving style. For brand new cars, costs are low or nonexistent due to your new car warranty. Generally, even larger costs may be covered up to 30,000 miles or 3 years. (some automakers have longer warranties).

By the time your car travels 60,000 miles (when most new car warranties have run out), you can be facing much larger bills. Depending on the make/model of your car, and the manufacturer recommends a 60,000 mile service, you need to have that service performed on your vehicle. If you fail to complete the service, you could potentially cost yourself thousands of dollars in the future.

My customers with older cars, often ask me if an expensive repair is worth it, given the value of their car. "Should I just buy a new car?", They ask. They often forget the expenses associated with a new car—increased registration fees and insurance, let alone car payments. These can be significant expenses.

In most cases, it's usually a better deal to repair your car versus buying something new. It might even be a better option to buy a different used car instead of fixing your older car in some cases.

There are many factors you'll need to take into account, like mileage, condition of your car and how long you plan to keep it. All this should be taken into consideration before you open your wallet.

## After reading this book you should:

- Understand the basics of car and maintenance.

- Learn how to keep accurate records.

- Learn how to pay attention to warning signs.

- Know what to ask to get the right help for your car.

## Let's get to know your car

Read your owner's manual. I know this may sound obvious, but it's surprising how many people don't, or won't. Little do they know the value of that book.

At *minimum*, you should know:

- What weight of oil does the manufacturer recommend for your car?

- Does your car take regular, synthetic or other type of oil?

- How many quarts of oil does your engine need?

- How often does the manufacturer recommend you change your oil? (see Chapter 2 for our recommendations)

- What are the correct tire pressures for each tire (some cars require different pressures from front to back).

- Type of fuel? Regular Unleaded, Premium or Diesel?

# About My Car (fill in the blanks)

Year: __________

Make: ________________________________

Model: ________________________________

Sub/Trim Model: ____________________________

☐ Rear wheel drive      ☐ Front wheel drive

☐ All wheel drive

Type of oil.

☐ 5w20  Regular

☐ 5w30  Synthetic Blend

☐ 10w30 Full Synthetic

☐ Other: ____________________________

Number of quarts your engine needs: __________

Tires: Some cars have different sizes on the front and the rear. Be sure to note that here:

Front: ________________ Rear: ____________________

Tire Brand: ____________________________

Recommended tire pressure as per manufacturer (sticker located inside of driver door frame and/or gas door):

Front: ________________ Rear: ____________________

Manufacturer's recommended fuel type

☐ Regular     ☐ Premium      ☐ Diesel

## Your Car Talks to You!
## You Need to Listen!

For people who drive their car every day, take the time to listen to your car and also get a *seat of the pants* feel for it. Over time, you'll become familiar with the way it starts, the feel of the brakes, the sounds it makes and yes, even the smells (you'd be surprised what car odors can tell you) while driving.

Once you've become familiar with how your cars sounds and feels, take note of any changes. Never ignore things your car may be trying to tell you. When something changes, it's generally only going to get worse, or even catastrophic.

Take notice if your car has any of these issues:

- Harder to start.

- Running a little hotter on the temperature gauge.

- Squeaking or grinding noises when you brake.

- Making a noise you're never heard your car make before.

- Producing weird smells associated with a noise.

- Feeling funny or loose while driving.

- Not braking like it used to - feeling mushy in the pedal.

- Has shaking in the steering wheel or pulls to one side.

- Squeals when turning the steering wheel.

- A check engine or other warning light on.

If you're experiencing any of the symptoms above, your car is trying to tell you something. Listen.

These are all warning signs. In particular, note when these things happen. Was the car hot or cold, were you at a stoplight, driving a neighborhood street or on the highway?

The more you can share with the shop, the better chance they have of duplicating any issues. Take your notes with you when you take your car to the shop.

The shop will probably charge you a diagnostic fee and that's fair, as you're paying for their time, training and expertise.

Taking your car to the shop BEFORE you have a bigger issue will save you lots of money, plus a potential tow bill.

For the auto repair shop to diagnose your car correctly, they will first test drive your car. It may be a good idea for you to go with the technician so you can both understand what you feel/hear/smell when driving your car.

## Maintenance Costs Less Than Repairs

The best way to minimize repair expenses is to keep current on the maintenance of your car. You want your car checked over at every oil change. You want to know what repairs are coming due.

Knowledge is power. Don't wait until something fails and you have to tow the car. Repairs will generally cost more than maintenance.

**Maintenance**, is a scheduled service. You make an appointment and you take your car into the shop. You are generally quoted up front how much the maintenance will cost you.

**Breakdowns,** are unscheduled repairs that seem to happen at the most inconvenient time; when you need to pick up your kids or get to work.

When a car has unexpected trouble, you most likely have to tow the car to the repair shop. When you consider the cost of a tow, missed time from work and being late to pick up your child, you can see how much a car breakdown really costs you in both time and money.

For most people, buying a car will be the largest or second-largest purchase they will make in their lifetime. Doesn't it make sense to educate yourself on how to take care of your car?

Taking your car to the auto shop shouldn't be a stressful experience, especially when you know what to ask. The auto shop owners and service writers want to be your trusted advisor and friend. It's always better to have an experienced friend on your side. When you know the right questions to ask and like the answers, you will better understand what you're spending money on.

Want to know more? Check out these FREE resources:

http://theautogirl.com/auto-care-for-women-downloads

# Chapter Two
## The Oil Change

*Relationships, like cars, should undergo regular services to make sure they are still roadworthy.*
*~ Zygmunt Bauman*

Your car's oil change should include an inspection.

So, you're probably wondering, WHY do I need to change my oil? What happens to it? My car isn't leaking, so I'm good, right?

Engine oil, whether mineral or synthetic based, contains additives that help your oil clean, cool, seal and lubricate all the moving parts in your engine. Over time, small bits of metal wear off, dirt that manages to get past your air filter, and foreign particles in gasoline will contribute to greater wear on the moving parts.

Some of the oil additives are detergents that help keep parts clean. When your oil gets too dirty, it must be replaced (along with the oil filter), otherwise the grit increases wear and will seriously decrease the life of your engine.

You should follow the recommended oil change intervals provided by your car's manufacturer.

Having your oil changed at regular intervals is the best thing you can do for your car. It used to be that oil changes were recommended every 3,000 miles. With today's better oils and tighter fitting engines, recommendations are now roughly 5,000-mile intervals for regular oil and 7,500-mile intervals for synthetic oil

Some automakers are recommending 10,000 miles for their new cars between oil changes. At my shop, we recommend oil changes at no more than 7,500 for these vehicles. We feel that 10,000 miles is too long. Oil additives break down and don't perform as well as they should. You may have spent a lot of money on your car, why chance it?

# Why You Want Your Car Looked Over at Every Oil Change

A friend's daughter brought her Honda Civic into the shop because steam was coming from the engine. After checking out the car, we determined her engine had a blown head gasket and her car would need an expensive repair.

She had always taken her car to one of those quick oil change places. While I am proud of her for getting the oil changed routinely, she could have prevented this break down by taking her car to a repair shop. The shop would have inspected her car at every oil change and would have told her the thermostat housing was leaking coolant. At that point, she could have replaced the housing and saved hundreds and not blown the head gasket. If she had continued to drive with no coolant, the engine would have likely seized, and she would have been looking at a repair of thousands of dollars.

I spent time to educate her that she needs her car inspected at every oil change. The quick lube oil changes may save you a few dollars in the short run but can cost you hundreds down the road. Most don't do a complete inspection on your car.

Quick lube shops may seem like a great way to get your oil changed quickly. Most of these shops do not perform repairs, they only recommend fluid exchanges.

They will try to sell you on new coolant, new brake fluid, power steering fluid, transmission and differential services.

A car with leaking coolant will have problems keeping the engine cool and will eventually overheat. You may think you're ok if you just keep adding water to the radiator, but you're only delaying the inevitable repair.

If you don't know what is going on with your car, it is the responsibility of a reputable repair shop to let you know. Whether or not you do the repair is up to you.

There's a difference between finding someone you trust and someone trying to sell you services you don't need.

## Arm yourself with knowledge

You don't need to change all these fluids every time you take your car in for an oil change.

Check your owner's manual. There you will find listings for changing fluids based on mileage intervals.

Most auto repair shops can also change your oil in about an hour. What you are missing at a quick lube shop is a thorough vehicle inspection.

Consider finding an auto repair shop that you can build a relationship with and take your car to the same place each time.

## A good shop will:

- Test drive your car before they perform any service or repairs.

- Discuss any issues you have with your vehicle.

- Check all fluids at every visit.

- Check tires pressures on every visit.

- Inspect your car for any current or upcoming issues and potential problems.

- Recommended Manufacturer's services that should be brought to your attention.

- Make sure all service lights on the dashboard are off.

- Notify you if your car has any active recalls.

By now, you should realize that having a basic understanding of your car and what it needs to be maintained, is an important tool when talking to a repair shop.

After a car inspection, discuss the shop's list of recommendations. Have them prioritize the list. Some repairs may need to be done right away, while others can be completed at a later date. You want a list of things that may be leaking, grinding or possibly cause your car to have trouble.

The job of a trusted auto repair shop is to keep your car running at the lowest operating cost possible. This can only be done by looking over the car EVERY time the car comes into the shop.

Keep records in your car and track your expenses. Most shops will keep records on your car as well, but it's good to compare.

What if you had a fluid changed last year, but don't have the records and you're going to a different place every time? You may be paying for a service you don't need.

# Knowledge is Power

Maintaining your car by servicing and repairing parts along the way will save you hundreds over the life of your car.

A car current on its scheduled maintenance will give you many safe years of driving. Many of today's cars are capable of taking you 200,000 miles! It's not  unheard of to go even further!

# Chapter Three
## Keep Accurate Records

*If GM had kept up with technology like the computer industry has, we would all be driving $25 cars that got 1,000 MPG.*
*~ Bill Gates*

I've touched on this earlier, but I want to further stress how important this can be. "Do I really need to keep my receipts if my shop keeps records?"

Yes, and for multiple reasons. For starters, you may be going to several different shops, each having different maintenance records. Being able to track your maintenance and repairs will help assure you're taking good care of your car.

Second, you'll save money by not paying for services/repairs you've already paid for.

Third, the receipts can help you keep track of your part warranties. When a part you have replaced fails, having the receipt available will get the part replaced under warranty.

Finally, when you do decide to sell your car, especially to a private buyer, it's an easier sale if the potential buyer knows you've taken good care of the car by including the receipts with the sale.

Here's an example of why it's a good idea to keep records:

Your car battery dies. You have it replaced, and eleven months later it's dead again. Do you even remember where you bought it? Is the battery defective, or has your charging system failed?

For many people, their first thought is they need a new battery. If you've kept the receipt, you'll know where you bought it, and when, so you'll be able to see how long the warranty is. If it's still under warranty, you may be able to get it replaced for free, or prorated, from the place you bought it.

Without a receipt, the shop may not go out of their way to look up your records, and try to sell you a new battery, so keep that receipt.

While writing this book, I got a call very early one morning from my daughter in New Orleans. I actually slept through the first call and heard the phone ringing the second time she called. "My car has a flat tire"! she exclaimed frantically, "and I've got to get to class soon, I can't miss this test!"

She explained that the right rear tire was flat and that she wanted to change the tire herself rather than call for help. I want to mention here that we recently had four new tires put on the car maybe 5 months ago.

She didn't want to call a tow truck. She hadn't changed a tire before and wanted me to walk her through the process. I had her open the trunk to find the spare, the jack and the lug wrench.

"There's no tire here!", she said. "Look under the trunk carpet to get to the spare tire compartment," I told her. There she found the spare and the tools needed to replace it.

I suggested that before she jacks up the car she needed to slightly loosen the lug nuts. "Use your body weight to step on the lug wrench," I explained. I then explained that she then needs to put the jack in front of the rear tire. There she will find a smooth spot underneath where she can put the jack. The jack must go there, or you can damage the car. She found the spot and was able to jack up the car. She finished taking off the lug nuts and removed the tire.

When she tried to put the spare tire on the car she realized that it wouldn't fit and that she would have to jack up the car a bit more. She was able to lift the spare onto the wheel studs. It wouldn't fit the first time and she realized that the tire was backwards. Once she switched it around it fit perfectly. She tightened the lug nuts.

She then lowered the jack and put it back in the car along with the flat tire. I explained that the tire shop would put the spare tire back where it goes after they patch it and put the tire on the car. Once the tire was back on the ground, she used her weight to tighten the lug nuts a bit more.

I was proud of my daughter! She was happy she was able to get the tire changed quickly even though her hands were dirty, and she didn't have any wipes to use. The rag in the trunk helped a little.

"Do you have the tire paperwork in your glove box?" I asked. She said she did, "Just like you taught me mom. Hmm, I purchased these tires almost 8 months ago, it's longer than I thought."

Fortunately, the shop where she bought the tires was nearby. She headed straight there and took her receipts in with her. They were able to patch the tire, check the air pressure in the spare and put it all back into the trunk. All at no charge! Had she gone to some random place for a flat repair, she might have been charged. Having the receipts with her saved her money.

She was able to get back on the road. She called me. "They didn't charge me for the tire repair!" She was off to take her test.

It really is so simple. If my daughter can change a tire, then so can yours.

## Do You Know Where Your Last Service Was Performed?

You should keep accurate records of services performed on your car. If you go to one repair shop and they perform a service, then months later you go to another shop and they recommend the same service, would you even know if you have had that service completed?

It's up to you to keep your receipts. Keeping the receipts in the glove box will keep them accessible when you need them. Get an envelope and keep all of your car repair receipts in one place, for easy reference.

Any car repair receipts stored in a file in your home will not help you when you are at a shop.

Keeping accurate records can save you hundreds of dollars.

Want to know more? Check out these FREE resources:

http://theautogirl.com/auto-care-for-women-downloads

# Chapter Four
## How to Find a Great Shop

*We want transportation as reliable as running water.*
*~ Travis Kalanick*

How Do You Find a Great Shop?

It's not as hard as you think. There are many great shops out there who are honest, have high standards and operate with integrity.

These shops have good reputations, stand by their work and will still be there the next time you need service.

Do some research and you will be able to make a great decision. You want to look for a shop that you feel comfortable with. One that will answer your questions, show you around the shop and who will give you honest answers.

Don't necessarily choose the shop with the lowest price. A good shop will want to see the car first. They cannot accurately diagnose over the phone. If the shop doesn't look over your car first and they quote a price, you may find that price will increase after they see your car. The lowest priced shops, often skimp on quality parts, have non-skill workers and may not even pay their employees fair wages.

Trained technicians don't come cheap. But think about it, who do you want to do your surgery? A guy who got his medical degree online or a highly trained, experienced doctor, who specializes in what ails you?

## Quality by Association

Look for shops that belong to an association. These shops keep up with the laws and have high ethical standards and help to elevate the auto repair industry.

I'm a member of the Automotive Service Council of California (ASCCA). These shop owners represent shops that want to make a difference. They are involved with the state of California legislatures and keep the members updated on all of the new laws. These members are watching out for the industry as a whole and for their customers.

There are many other associations as well that are making a great impact on the auto repair industry. A few of these include: ASA, Auto Care Association, ASE, Women in Auto Care, and NASTF.

## Some Advice When Looking for a Repair Shop to Service Your Vehicle

Ask your friends or co-workers for a recommendation. See if they can give you a good referral to a shop that they trust and use regularly.

Search for a shop near your work or home. Talk to the owner. Many independent shops are run by the owner who will be happy to give you a tour and show their facility.

If you're trying to find a good shop for yourself, look online at reviews. Drive by the shop and see how clean they are. Look at their waiting room and the cleanliness of the garage.

Ask questions. Ask about a repair or service that you need. See how well they answer your questions.

If you have a good feeling, give the shop the opportunity to earn your business. Look around the shop. Many owners love to talk with their customers. Find one who is happy to get to know you and your concerns about your car.

The dealer is not always better. Dealers have huge overhead costs and charge a higher rate than most independent shops and often have shorter warranties. Independent shops can buy parts from aftermarket sources that have better warranties and better prices than the dealer.

## Why Women Don't Ask Questions

Throughout my years in business, I hear horrible car stories from women who often feel intimidated by service advisors.

Why is this? Generally, it's because they don't know much about their car, they don't know what questions to ask and even if they ask a few questions, they often don't know if the service or repair being sold is actually needed or not.

## What the Repair Shop Should Tell You

You should be told that they need to diagnose your car before quoting you a price.

Just because someone else tells you what may be wrong does not necessarily mean that the part needs to be replaced.

Let the shop diagnose your car and give you a complete recommendation. After all, that is what they are trained and qualified to do. You should be told what is wrong with your car and why. You should get details of what part had an issue and what needs to be done to repair the problem.

Good shops include good warranties. This should include a parts and labor warranty.

## Questions You Should Ask

What part failed and why?

Does this need to be replaced now or can I wait until a later date?

What other parts need to be replaced?

How long will the repair take?

What type of warranty do you offer?

What will happen if the repair isn't done today?

The shop should not pressure you into paying for the job at that moment. They should answer your questions and make you feel at ease. They should offer to show you the old parts. They should show you the problem on your car.

Ask questions until you understand. Never decide based on pressure from the shop.

Great shops don't pressure you. They inform and educate. It's your car, it's your choice.

If the shop says you should not drive the car in that condition, then they will let you know.

Remember, some repairs can be completed at a later date, but there are some repairs that need to be performed or the car might not be safe.

## How do I know if my car needs a recommend repair?

One of the most common questions asked is that the customer wants to know if they really need are commended repair, especially if it's expensive. In their mind, their car is running fine. It may be, but as I've illustrated earlier, something like a coolant leak may not affect how your car is running, until it overheats and possibly causes major damage.

I can't stress enough how important it is to listen to your car—to feel your car. Far too many people ignore the signs and end up spending lots of money at the repair shop.

If you play the radio in your car every time you drive, try turning it off once in a while. Listen for any new noises that you may not have heard before. And yes, notice if anything smells weird too!

# Can You Relate to These Customers?

One day, Violet came by the shop on a recommendation from a good customer. Her husband, who had taken care of all their car maintenance, had passed away six months before. Violet wasn't sure what to do.

She had recently taken her car to the dealer for an oil service and they told her that the power steering rack was leaking, and the repair would cost $1,300. She was uneasy about spending that kind of money, so she didn't have the dealer fix her car.

Talking with her neighbor about her car's issue, he suggested that she take her car to my shop. She made an appointment and brought the car in for us to inspect. My technicians found no leaking or noise, or any issue caused by the steering rack at the time. Was the dealer trying to take advantage of her or just a misdiagnosis? Checking in with her two months later, she was still not having any car issues.

What Violet did right was to take her car to another shop to get a second opinion. You don't have to pay for everything the shop is trying to sell you. You have the right to get a second opinion.

One day in May, Janine made an appointment at my shop to have her brakes replaced. A month prior, another shop told her she needed brakes. In preparation, Janine provided us with her car's VIN so we could have the parts here ready to go.

After checking in, my technician took the car for a test drive and put the car on the lift for a brake inspection. The technician took measurements and found the pads still had 6 mm on both the front and the rear.

We brought her back into the shop to show her the brake pads and explain that it wasn't quite time to replace the brakes. There was still plenty of life left on those pads!

Generally, you replace pads when they are down to 3-4 mm. She did not need to replace brakes that day. She thanked us for being honest and saving her money.

I share these stories because they illustrate what can happen and what you can do to make sure you are only paying for repairs that you need.

These stories have become all too familiar in the auto repair industry. Even though there are many honest shops, we don't hear much about them. People like to share when they are unhappy. An unhappy customer will tell most everyone they know.

Don't make decisions based on pressure from anyone. This is your car and you have the right to get the repair done or take your car to another shop for a second opinion.

Remember, ask the right questions and feel good about the decisions you make. Find a good shop that you can trust and build a relationship with them.

# Chapter Five
## How to Check Vital Fluids

*There's no harm in hoping for the best as long as you're prepared for the worst*
*~ Stephen King*

## Check Your Car BEFORE You Have an Issue

As the driver, you are responsible to make sure that you have oil in your engine, coolant in your radiator and the proper air pressures in your tires.

Other fluids, like the transmission fluid in your transmission, power steering fluid in the steering box or gear oil in the transfer case in a

4-wheel-drive vehicle are often more difficult to check but should be checked regularly by your shop.

If you don't want to check these fluids, then you need to find an auto repair shop that will do it for you.

It is important to check levels because fluids can leak out through gaskets and hoses onto parts of the car below the leak.

Leaking fluids may not hit the driveway or your parking space, so you can't use the spots as an indication that fluid is leaking. By then it may be too late.

Many cars have plastic under-shields that can hold the dripping fluids, so you may be unaware a fluid is leaking.

Low fluid levels can damage vital parts. Fluids should be kept at their optimal levels. Therefore, it is so important to have your car looked at on a regular basis.

Either schedule a monthly (by-monthly, quarterly, etc) day and time to check your own fluids or schedule a routine oil service to have these fluids checked for you. Set a reminder on your phone.

# How to Check the Oil Level in Your Engine

You will need a rag or paper towel.

If your oil reading is low, you will also need:

Oil - as recommended by the manufacturer of your car and a Funnel.

Oil should be checked when your engine is cold or hasn't been running for at least 30 minutes.

Make sure your car is on level ground, or as near to level as you find.

Open the hood of your car. Consult your owner's manual for the location of the lever. Once you have pulled the lever, you will need to release the secondary safety lever at the front of the hood. This may be located near the center - and you will either need to lift the lever up or push down depending on your car.

Your owner's manual will explain this. Some cars have a hood support rod you will need to attach as described in your car's owner manual. This will keep your hood propped open.

Locate the oil dipstick on the engine. Pull out the dipstick and wipe off the oil with your rag.

Re-insert the dipstick. Make sure it's all the way in.

Pull out the dipstick and look at the marks for full and low. The oil level should be within the range between FULL and ADD. These areas will be clearly marked.

If the oil level appears below the ADD mark, you may need to add some oil. Repeat the steps above to make sure the first check was accurate.

## If you need to add oil

On the top of your engine you will find a cap labeled OIL. You will need to twist this off.

Insert the funnel into the oil fill tube. Pour only a portion of the quart in.

Re-check the dipstick before adding more oil. You do not want to overfill.

Once the oil reaches the full level, put the oil cap back on. Don't forget this part!

Put the lid back on the quart of oil and store in your car.

NOTE: Some newer cars may not have a dipstick.

If your car does not have a dipstick, check your owner's manual. You may need to check the oil level electronically on your dashboard.

NOTE: If you consistently find between oil changes that your oil level is low, let your auto shop know sooner rather than later, as this may be in indication of an impending problem or failure.

## Checking your Coolant Level

This can be checked when your engine is hot OR cold, however, it's safer to check when cold.

**CAUTION: NEVER TAKE THE COOLANT CAP OFF OF THE RADIATOR WHEN THE ENGINE IS HOT AS IT MAY RESULT IN SERIOUS BURNS!**

Open the hood of your car. Consult your owner's manual for the location of the lever.

Once you have pulled the lever, you will need to release the secondary safety lever at the front of the hood. This may be located near the center - and you will either need to lift the lever up or push down depending on your car. Your owner's manual will explain this. Some cars have a hood support rod you will need to attach as described in your car's owner manual. This will keep your hood propped open.

With most modern cars, you won't be checking the coolant level in your radiator—you will be checking the coolant recovery bottle. This cloudy-colored bottle is almost always located to one side or the other, near a front fender. You will see two marks molded into the bottle - HOT and COLD. If you're just turned your car off after a trip and are checking, the fluid should be close to the HOT indicator.

If you haven't run your car for a while, this level should appear near the COLD indicator. If you see NO fluid in the recovery bottle, you may need to add coolant. If you decide you need to add coolant, it's extremely important you use the correct coolant recommended by the automaker. The wrong type may damage your cooling system.

Fresh coolant can be added directly into the coolant recovery bottle. Use a funnel to keep from spilling Antifreeze, as it can damage your car's finish. Many antifreeze solutions are also toxic, and if spilled on the ground may harm animals.

Pour in enough coolant to bring the level up to the cold mark (if your engine is cold) on the recovery bottle.

In an emergency - you can use water if Antifreeze isn't available - however, you will probably throw off the proper mixture of Antifreeze and water. In this circumstance, you will want to visit your shop as soon as it's convenient to have them check the mixture. Too much water will damage your cooling system.

Coolant systems do not normally need coolant added. This is a closed system which means that the coolant circulates throughout the radiator and hoses and the fluid should remain at the same level.

If you consistently find your coolant low, you should schedule an appointment with the auto repair shop because there is a reason, and you need to know.

## How to Check Your Tires Air Pressure

Most moderately-priced tires today will last anywhere from 30,000 to 50,000 miles before they need to be replaced. Your mileage will vary depending on your car, it's condition and to a large extent, your driving style.

So, if the correct tire pressure is so important, how do I check it? How do I know what the correct pressure should be?

Before you check your tire pressure, you first need to know what the correct tire pressure should be. This information is located on a sticker located in the door jam of your car, usually the driver's door, but not always. It may also be located in the fuel door, on the trunk lid or on glove box door.

You can purchase a tire pressure gauge and any local parts supply store. It should cost you roughly $10-15.

Tire pressure is measured in Pounds Per Square inch (PSI).

NOTE: Some cars have different PSI for front versus rear tires so check on that.

To check tire pressure, unscrew the valve stem cap on your tire, put the tire pressure gauge into the valve stem and press down quickly to get a reading. This will cause the stick inside the gauge to slide out. This will mark the current pressure in your tire. If the reading is too low you need to add air to your tire.

## How to Add Air to Your Tires

Most people don't have ready access to compressed air. In many places in the US you can find air filling stations at most gas stations. If you can't find one, go to your nearest auto shop or tire shop. They will often check and add air for free.

If you do have access to compressed air, remove the valve stem cap, and in the same manner as you checked the pressure, push the air nozzle on to the valve stem, and push the lever to add air to the tire. Count off a few seconds and use your tire gauge to check the pressure. Add air as needed to get to the correct pressure. Try to get as close as you can to the correct pressure.

If you overfill the tire, you can press on the stem inside the tire valve to let some air out.

Remember, put the stem cover back on the valve stem. The cover is important as it keep out dirt and debris that might push down on the center stem, letting out air. Check your tires often for missing covers and replace when missing.

## Keep An Eye On Your Tires

Have you ever seen those pieces of tire on the side of the highway? As I drive by them, I wonder how the driver handled the blowout of the tire. Did they swerve all over the road before coming to a stop on the side of the highway, or plow into another car?

What happened to cause the tire to blowout in the first place?

One major reason for blowouts is an under-inflated tire. Under-inflated tires will cause portions of the sidewall to touch the pavement.

Sidewalls were not meant to be driven on, and will fail.

According to the National Highway Traffic Safety Administration, under-inflated tires have a higher risk of damage and failure. Your tires will also wear out faster if under-inflated. There is also a bigger chance of a tire blowout.

The other major reason is a foreign object (nail, screw, random piece of metal) puncturing your tire. This is more likely to happen if your tires are past their wear limits.

Tires have a thickness that wears out over time. Every road tire sold in the USA will have wear indicators molded into the tread (the grooves) of the tire. These perpendicular bars will become level with your tread when the tire has reached its useful life. If you continue to drive on worn-out tires, you're risking tire failure and possibly an accident.

**CAUTION: Worn out tires are extremely dangerous on wet roads.**

## Check Your Wiper Blades

Wiper blades are perhaps the most overlooked car care items, yet they are extremely important to safe driving. You want to be able to see out your windshield, don't you?

Over time, wiper blades dry out as well as wear and then start to fall apart. This leads to smearing of the dirt on the windshield. If left to go too long, can even scratch your windshield. (Some windshields can be very expensive!)

Wipers should be replaced when they get too dry. As a general rule, replace once a year, or more often in hot, dry areas.

Want to know more? Check out these FREE resources:

http://theautogirl.com/auto-care-for-women-downloads

# Chapter Six
## Let's Get Detailed

*We think in generalities, but we live in detail*
*~ Alfred North Whitehead*

It's beyond the scope of this book to get too technical, so I'll try to keep this fairly simple for those who want to know more.

## First, the Fluids

Fluids are vital to the care and maintenance of your car. These fluids keep your car operating in tiptop shape. Changing these vital fluids once in a while is not a bad thing. Check your owner's manual for a schedule of when these should be done.

**Coolant** runs through your engine keeping everything at the optimal operating temperature. As it passes through the front radiator, it cools off and then passes through the hot motor to collect heat and return back to the radiator to cool off. A running engine constantly cycles coolant.

Coolant consists of a mixture of antifreeze and water and contains rust inhibitors that help keep the cooling channels and hoses clear of rust that can damage the cooling system.

Coolant, despite its name, also provides the heat in your car on those cold mornings. Next to oil, this is probably the second-most important fluid in your car.

Your coolant should be changed at the mileage called for in your owner's manual. This range is anywhere from 30,000 to 60,000 miles. Some automakers won't cover the cost of replacing coolant under warranty, as they consider this to be a lifetime fluid.

All fluids break down over time and should be replaced at some point. Talk to your shop for their recommendation.

**Power steering fluid** is necessary to run the power steering pump that assists your steering wheel. Like engine oil, it also helps clean, cool, seal and lubricate the working parts of the pump. Just like coolant, it can leak at some point. You want to have the hoses and the fluid levels checked.

**Transmission fluid** helps cool the internal parts of the transmission and keep it shifting smoothly. This fluid also gets heated while driving and degrades over time. You may get a longer transmission life by changing out the transmission fluid at regular intervals.

**Brake fluid** is necessary to keep the brakes working smoothly. Brake fluid transmits the force you apply with your foot, through the brake lines, to the brake cylinders, which apply force to the brake pads, to stop your car. If you notice the brake pedal not working correctly or feeling too soft, you need to have your brakes checked immediately.

Changing this fluid from time to time can help keep your brakes working properly.

Brake fluid is hygroscopic, which means it attracts moisture. Over time, your brake fluid will become contaminated with water, which can attack the metal components that make up your braking system. Check your owner's manual for a schedule of when this should be done.

Differential fluid. If your car has a differential, you need to have the fluid checked. Some cars have sealed units. Check your manufacturer's recommended schedule to see how often they recommend a differential fluid service.

# Other Mechanical and Electrical Systems

## Brake System

Brakes wear out over time. New brake pads are approximately 12-mm thick. When the brakes get to 3mm, the brake wear sensors may let you know by making noise or squealing. Some cars have electronic sensors. Not all cars have brake sensors. However, you shouldn't rely only on the sensors, as they sometimes fail.

You need to change your brake pads when they get to 3-mm, otherwise you run the risk of scratching the brake rotors. If there are deep grooves in the rotors, they may need to be replaced as well.

Brake rotors are also measured by thickness. Each manufacturer has a minimum thickness for the brake rotors. Sometimes the rotors can just be resurfaced. This only happen if there is enough thickness on the pads after the resurfacing. When the rotors wear to the minimum measurement, it's time to change the brake rotors also.

## Charging System

The charging system consists of a mechanical device called an alternator that runs off a belt on the front of your engine. Think of an alternator as an electric motor, except it makes electricity instead of using electricity. The alternator charges your car's battery. The battery is what stores the power necessary to run the starter that initially cranks over the engine to get it running. Once the engine is running, the alternator takes over all your car's electrical needs, from headlights to the radio and everything in between. While your drive, it also continues to keep your battery charged for the next time you need to start your car.

Dead batteries are one of the top reasons for car trouble. Batteries don't last forever and will need to be replaced at some point. Sometimes it's a faulty battery, but often it's your charging system that is failing to keep your battery fully charged.

The symptoms of a dying battery show up suddenly. Your car cranks over slowly or fails to crank at all. In this case, you'll need to get a jump-start to get going. If you can, head straight to your mechanic and explain the situation. They can test both the strength of your battery, as well as how well your charging system is working.

# Engine Basics

Your car's engine is made up of hundreds of moving parts that work in unison. There are also many other mechanical, electrical, and computer-controlled devices that are designed to help the engine run. The failure of some of these parts may only cause small issues, while the failure of some components can cost you thousands.

We've covered this earlier, but I can't stress enough how important clean oil is for your engine's health.

Parts can and will wear out, break, burn out or otherwise fail to function. Hoses can and will leak or burst. Parts can become loose, causing gaskets to leak.

Auto technicians are trained to spot potential problems BEFORE you're stranded on the side of the road.

Due to the complexity of modern cars, most shops use an inspection sheet, so they can thoroughly check over your car's engine and other items so as to not miss anything.

One sign that you may have engine trouble is when the car starts to run rough. Sometimes the check engine light will come on, but sometimes it won't.

# Timing Belt

On many modern cars, your service advisor may tell you around 60,000 miles that your car is due for a timing belt replacement. What is a timing belt and why do I need to replace it?

Without getting too technical, a timing belt is an internal engine belt that is connected to many moving parts that must be in perfect sync in order for the engine to run properly. This belt wears and stretches over time and can cause these items to run out of sync. Because the wear and stretch happen slowly, you probably won't notice your engine isn't running the same as it used to.

What happens if I don't replace the timing belt?

Often, people are reluctant to incur the cost of $400-600 (on average) to have this service performed if they feel their car is running fine.

Depending on the type of engine you have, this can be a very costly mistake.

Some engines are known as *Interference Motors*.

This is because if your timing belt breaks, the movement of these internal parts will interfere with each other and will cause parts to bend and/or break, costing you potentially thousands of dollars to fix. In worst-case scenarios, you could be looking at a complete engine replacement.

Non-interference motors generally won't break internally if the timing belt snaps, however, there can be other minor engine damage that occurs. While a cheaper repair, it's still MUCH more expensive than replacing the timing belt per the automakers recommendation. Consult your owner's manual for specifics.

## Transmissions

An automatic transmission has a torque converter that connects your engine to your transmission. The transmission shifts gears based on the speed of the car.

Manual transmissions are operated by shifting gears with your hand, whereas, a clutch separates the engine from the transmission when you depress the clutch pedal. The clutch uses friction materials similar to brakes, will wear out over time, and will need to be replaced at some point. Clutches usually last a long time, however, this depends greatly on your driving style.

Transmission require forms of lubrication to run correctly, although they each require different types of fluid. At some point, a transmission will experience some trouble. You will notice the car getting stuck in a gear or a rough shifting into the next gear.

Follow your manufacturer's recommended schedule for servicing the transmission fluid.

Only use fluid recommend by the manufacturer. Using the wrong fluid can cause damage to the internal workings of the transmission.

# Chapter Seven
## Cars are an Expense

*Confidence comes from being prepared*
*- John Wooden*

## So, you want a new (or new to you) car?

Let's take a look at the options:

- Buy a new car from a dealer.

- Buy a certified used car from a dealer.

- Buy a used car from a private party.

- Lease a Car

# Buying a New Car

**Advantages:**

- You get a warranty (these days, usually 50,000 miles, though some automakers go even higher).

- Easier to maintain, less repair cost with the low miles.

- Latest styling and color you want.

- All the features you want.

**Disadvantages:**

- Car depreciates quickly (loses value once driven off showroom floor).

- Car insurance, sales taxes on total price and state licensing fees are expensive.

# Buying a Certified Used Car

**Advantages:**

- Less expensive than a new car (usually only 3-4 years old).

- Most have low mileage (lease returns or demo models).

- Can probably find one with most of the features you want.

- Comes with warranty, or you can opt to pay extra for one.

- Car insurance, sales taxes on total price and state licensing fees are cheaper than new.

**Disadvantages:**

- May be more costly than a used car from a private party.

- May not be able to find one with the options/color you want.

# Buying a Used Car

**Advantages:**

- Save money on purchase (much of the depreciation has already occurred).

- May have long life with this car, if well maintained.

- Can often find a car with more options at better price.

- Car insurance, sales taxes on total price and state licensing fees less on an older car.

**Disadvantages:**

- Reduced chance of getting all of your options or color you're looking for.

- Takes a little longer to find the car you want.

- Often doesn't come with any service history from previous owner.

## Leasing a Car

Do plenty of research before you choose this option. Don't get suckered into a monthly payment just because you can afford it. For most people, this is the most expensive way to obtain a car. People who choose this option do so for very specific reasons, usually as a business expense. (But only your tax professional can advise you on this). You technically never own this car. You make payments, taxes on payments, pay insurance and licensing fees. At the end of the lease, you return the car. You retain no value and have nothing to show for it.

**Advantage:**

- You can return at lease end and get another one.

- You can select your options on the car.

**Disadvantage:**

- You never own the car, so you have nothing to sell when you no longer want it.

- If you drive over allotted mileage, you pay a premium for the extra miles driven.

# What Car Should You Buy?
## Some things to think about:

- What are some of the options you can't live without?

- Do you want an automatic or a manual transmission?

- Do you prefer memory seats?

- Built-in navigation with integrated telephone?

- Rear-view camera?

- Cloth or leather seats?

- What other features do you want?

## Some Additional Things to Consider

Do you want a 2-door or 4-door? Would you want a sedan, truck, SUV or minivan? Have a family with small children?  Shy away from 2-doors (you'll thank me later).

Do you want a 4-, 6- or 8-cylinder car?  More cylinders have more power but cost more in gas and maintenance. Larger engines generally cost more to service and repair.

Cars with 4 cylinders get better gas mileage, so consider the gas mileage and cost to fill that tank weekly and multiply that times 52 weeks. This will give you an estimate for your annual fuel cost.

Check with your insurance company to see how much it will cost to insure the car. Know this before you buy. Rates can vary and it's better to ask ahead of time. You may be surprised, and not in a good way.

**A few more things to consider:**

European cars (Mercedes, Audi, BMW, MINI and Porsche) will cost more to maintain and repair.

A black car is a lot harder to keep clean and becomes a rolling oven in hot climates.

Think about naming your car. Many MINI owners do this. My MINI was named Bruiser.

Many people don't like to drive manual cars, especially going uphill or in traffic.

Convertible Volkswagen Beetles have big blind spots when looking over your shoulder. I named mine, *Blindspot!*

The most popular car color in the USA is white.

Want to know more? Check out these FREE resources:

http://theautogirl.com/auto-care-for-women-downloads

# Chapter Eight
## Buying a Used Car

*Before everything else, getting ready is the secret to success.*
*~ Henry Ford*

## People Keep Their Cars Longer Than They Think They Will

When someone buys a car, whether it's new or pre-owned, they tend to keep their car for a long time.

The last time I saw the statistic, I was surprised to read that the average car is 11 years old. Newer cars actually last longer than they used to and are more reliable.

To achieve the lowest operating cost for your vehicle, you should plan to keep your car for a long time.

It can be an exciting time when you decide to buy a car, however, the actual process often is not what you expect. It isn't really a pleasant experience. This is especially true if you are unexperienced in financial matters. Unscrupulous car salespeople may take advantage of you and you later realize you've made a bad deal.

Here's a story that happened to a friend, years ago. The first time she bought a used car from a dealer she let her excitement get the best of her. When negotiating the deal, she was so focused on getting the best price on her trade-in vehicle she didn't pay as much attention to negotiating a better price for the used car that she was buying.

Days later, after her excitement wore off, she realized that she had basically given them her old car. (she paid a bit too much for the newer car). By then of course, it was too late. The deal was done.

If you decide to trade in a car when you're buying another car, remember this - there is no such thing as TWO GOOD DEALS. You may get a good deal on what you're buying OR on your trade-in. Never BOTH.

When deciding to buy a used car, ask yourself, how financially savvy are you? If you're inexperienced, take someone with you who's done this before. You may just save yourself thousands of dollars.

## Used Car Dealer versus Private Party

### Used Car Purchased from a Dealership

Try to stick to brand name dealerships (Ford, Mercedes, Honda, Toyota, etc...) if you don't mind paying a little more for the advantage of buying a higher quality used car. Generally, dealers only keep their better trade-ins for resale and auction-off the rest. Their cars will often be newer, will have fewer upcoming maintenance and/or repair needs and may still have some of the original factory warranty left. They also offer extended warranties.

The trade-in cars they auction off have been deemed too expensive to repair for them to make a good profit.

### Corner Lot Used Car Dealers

This is often where the Dealer cars that are auctioned off end up. These lots have lower operating costs. It costs them less to make the necessary repairs on their inventory and still make a profit. There isn't necessarily anything wrong buying a car from these places but know that they often have older cars. The advantage, of course, is price. Generally, the cars are less expensive and often offer a good value.

## Car Buying Mistake #1

Car salespeople know EXACTLY how most people buy cars. Emotionally. Oh, yes. I know what you're thinking, "I don't do that. I use logic and only buy what I need." Well, you may be the exception, but most people put themselves in a vulnerable spot when looking at that shiny car.

They imagine flying down the road, wind in their hair, friends in the back seat and the radio blasting their favorite tunes. It's a nice dream - but SNAP out of it!! This is your wallet on the line! Don't let sales people take advantage of your emotions.

## Car Buying Mistake #2

Unless you're paying cash for the whole amount, you're financing this purchase. Many people shopping for a used car determine what car they will buy based on how much they can afford to pay per month. If this is your only criteria, you'll probably end up regretting your purchase when you find out how long you have to pay for it.

You need to look at the financing of the car and what the total with interest will cost you at the end of the loan. Know what the interest rate will be. Check several financing options for the best interest rate. Maybe you can put more money down to qualify for a better rate. Check it out before you buy.

## Private Party Used Car

Once you decide on a car or two you want to buy, DO SOME RESEARCH on the Internet. Determine what features are a must, and what options are just nice to have. You can get a fairly accurate price range for the car you want - but be willing to compromise, as your selection may be limited. You might end up paying for features you don't need, but in the end, you get the car you want.

When going out to see a car from a private party, it's best to bring someone with you who has experience. Ask lots of questions! Once you get an owner talking, you'll be surprised what they'll tell you about their car.

Ask why they are selling. Are they buying another similar car, just newer, or are they buying something that is better on gas or costs less to repair?

Ask a lot of questions and listen to the answers. Find out how long they have owned the car. If the seller has driven the car for a long period of time, that is a good sign. If is sounds like the seller has not had the car long, then that is a red flag.

Look over the car for any broken items. Non-working items like air-conditioning or a broken taillight may cost a lot of money to repair. Take note of the mileage on the car. Many cars need a tune-up at 100k miles. This could include expensive labor hours and/or expensive parts. Any upcoming maintenance or repairs not performed may become an expensive repair for you. Ask for all copies of receipts for repairs and maintenance that have been done on the car.

Make sure the registration tags are current. It can be expensive to bring a car's registration current at the DMV, especially if the car hasn't been registered for awhile.

In some states, including California, it is the seller's responsibility to get the smog certificate before the sale can take place. The car must pass smog in order to transfer the title. This is a good thing. If the car cannot pass smog, repairs can possibly cost a lot of money, and that is the seller's responsibility. This really does protect the buyer from buying a car that needs repairing.

# What is a Salvage Title Car?

There are many cars for sale with a salvage title. Salvage title cars have been in an accident and the total damage exceeds a certain percentage of the value of the car (ranging from 75-90 percent). The insurance company will decide that it is not economically feasible to repair the car and declares the car a "total loss." This doesn't necessarily mean the car is damaged beyond repair.

The DMV will issue a **Salvage Certificate** to that car. Usually, the insurance company sells the car to either a repair facility or parts dismantler. If the car is repaired, most states require that it pass a basic safety inspection before the DMV issues a new title. This title is labeled as **Salvaged** so future owners are aware of it's past.

Many people buy salvage title cars and never have an issue. Others have mechanical problems. Also note that it is much tougher to sell a salvage title car. So think ahead before buying one. You can get auto insurance on a salvage titled car.

# Get a Pre-Purchase Inspection

If deciding to buy a used car from a corner lot or a private party, the best thing you can do is to take your car to an auto repair shop that offers a Pre-Purchase Inspection (PPI). This can cost around $100 or more, depending on the type of car.

The shop will look over the car for leaks and any potential issues. They will let you know what services are coming due. Make sure they take the car for a test drive, too, as this can help eliminate any drivability issues. This is money well spent.

After receiving a clean inspection or an inspection that shows minimal issues, you are then free to make an offer on the car. At this point, you will have a good feeling of the value of the car and what, if any, repairs you may need to take care of sooner than later. You can use these costs to help negotiate the selling price.

The extra precautions you take will help you to make the right decision when purchasing a used car.

To know what you are buying ahead of time will save you from the heartache and headache of buying a car that will be trouble.

An informed buyer makes their decision based on facts and not emotions.

Once you settle on a car to buy you won't have any buyer's remorse, so crank up the tunes, invite some friends and take a road trip!

# When I Bought a Used Car for My Son

When my oldest child, Tyler, was in New Orleans attending medical school, he was driving his old Mustang that had been back and forth across the country. He was driving home from class one day and the car started getting hot. He couldn't pull over right away and the car overheated. The temperature gauge hit the red zone.

He called me to ask what to do. I told him to take it to the nearest auto shop. They told him he needed to replace the head gasket, which was a big repair.

After discussing the situation, I knew it was best to sell the car based on the high mileage and get him into something more dependable. He would be in New Orleans for four years and I didn't want to get this call again!

Tyler was able to sell the Mustang for a few hundred dollars. I wanted to find him a car that he would like to drive. He chose a Honda Civic. He wanted a black car with a manual transmission.

That shouldn't be to difficult I thought. My sister, Stephanie, helped me search. She loves the thrill of the hunt!  We started researching Honda Civics. We drove around checking out several Hondas.

We kept searching and before long we found one through an ad that was a good match. My sister called them and discussed the car. She knew it was the perfect car for several reasons. They just had a baby and bought a bigger Honda. They had service records. The car was just what Tyler wanted.

The car was close by so my sister drove over to see it. She liked what she saw, so we arranged for the car to be brought to my shop, so we could perform a PPI.

Well, the car was in great shape. It was a black manual Honda Civic, 2-door with roll-up windows. Perfect for a medical school student. It was exactly what we were looking for. They accepted our offer and the car was ours.

Now, to perform some preventative main-tenance before the car headed out to Louisiana. The car had 98,342 miles. We changed the oil, replaced the coolant, changed the timing belt and replaced the spark plugs. The car was good to go.

Tyler flew out for a visit and drove the car back to New Orleans. Myles, one of my other sons drove out with him. The car has lasted through Tyler's five years in New Orleans.

He has since moved to Los Angeles for his first year of residency. My daughter Hilary is now in New Orleans driving the Honda.

The car only has 120,234 miles on it. The car has been very reliable, and the purchase was a big success.

Hilary has only had to replace the car battery and four tires. This car only needs to last her two more years. The plan is to drive the Honda home when she graduates from medical school. I am looking forward to another road trip!

# Chapter Nine
## Common Reasons for Car Trouble

*Everything in life is somewhere else, and you get there in a car.*
*~E. B. White*

## Car Trouble Happens When You Don't Have the Time

Paige was driving her 2005 BMW 330i home from work one day. She was selling her car and just had the car detailed.

As she started her last uphill drive towards home, she noticed that the temperature gauge on the car started to get hot. She found a safe place along the highway and pulled the car to the side of the road.

There she was, on the side of the highway, just as the sun was setting and the sky was getting dark. She didn't have a phone charger or her sweater. She had taken everything out of her car. She was not prepared.

At that time, she didn't know what was wrong. Paige explained that she did have several phone numbers of tow companies stored in her phone. Her first call was to her boyfriend to tell her where she was and that she would be home late. The second call was to the tow company. It took them 1 1/2 hours to send a tow truck. She had no choice but to wait in the dark.

The tow company arrived and towed her car back to the shop. She did have a credit card with which to pay her tow bill. Her boyfriend had arrived just in time to pick her up and get the two bills paid.

(Later she found out that the water pump she had replaced six months ago was leaking.)

Breakdowns happen when you least expect them. You should ALWAYS be prepared for car trouble.

# Most Common Reasons
# for Car Trouble

## Lost Keys

Misplacing or locking your key in the car makes it to the top of the list of why drivers get stranded.

For older cars (pre-1990) without electronic key fobs, consider buying a hide-a-key box. This small magnetic box can hold a key and be placed under your car in a hidden area. Then, when you need a key, it is where you need it to be.

Another option is to get a spare key (or two) made. Keep one with your car and give one to a significant other or a friend.

Newer cars tend to have more expensive electronic keys. They can open the car door and start the car in some models. These keys are expensive and not as easy to get a spare key made.

Special keys can only be made at the dealership because they need to be programed to your car. You will need to provide the title of your car along with your driver's license to get a spare key made.

If you have a newer car, you may have a service from the automaker who can unlock your car remotely.

Brand new cars will often come with a limited-time service, but you can continue this service for a fee.

Most major brands offer some sort of service. (OnStar, etc...).

## Dead Battery

At the first sign of a failing battery, have a charging system check performed. If the alternator is not working correctly, it can't charge your battery correctly. If the battery isn't being charged correctly, it will fail.

Most good batteries come with a warranty. Read the warranty to know how long the life of the battery should be. After 3-5 years, you may start to notice some issues such as dim headlights or dome light or electrical items running at a slower rate of speed. This is a symptom of a failing battery or charging system.

You need to pay attention when you start your car. If you notice any type of cranking or slow start issues, get these systems checked out sooner, rather than later.

# Engine Trouble

Engine trouble can happen at any time. We all know that engines are made up of many systems that allow your car to operate correctly. When one of these items wear out or stop working, the part will need to be replaced before the car is safe to drive.

Belts can break and not allow the pulleys to work correctly. Hoses can burst causing fluids to leak. Spark plugs can misfire, pulleys can seize up, radiators can leak, and bearings can screech.

If you don't feel your car is safe to drive, it's always advisable to tow your car to a repair shop.

Many things can happen to the engine if you continue to drive without knowing what's wrong.

Occasionally turn down your radio and listen to your car. Get to know the noises it makes. If you take the time to pay attention to your engine, you will most likely know when something doesn't sound right or when something doesn't feel right. This is the time to take your car to the repair shop, before something happens that can cause you to get stuck on the side of the road.

# Transmission Issues

When your car has transmission problems you will know it.

The car won't shift gears smoothly. Maybe you feel a clunk between gears, and sometimes the car gets stuck in gear.

Your transmission is made up of many moving parts that must work together.

Check with your auto repair shop to see if they recommend replacing the fluid in your transmission.

Usually this is done before a certain mileage. If there are too many miles on the transmission and the transmission starts to act funny, then changing the transmission fluid at that point will not help.

Make sure that the correct transmission fluid is used with your car. Always base the choice of fluid on the manufacturer's recommendation.

Newer CVT transmissions require a special transmission fluid.

Because there is no one correct answer to transmission issues and required fluids, this decision is best left to an experienced repair shop.

# Braking Issues

Brakes are a wear item. This means that as you brake, the pads wear down and so do the rotors.

Many cars have electronic brake wear sensors. A brake warning light will appear on your dash when the sensor indicates that the brake pads are low. Don't always rely on the brake warning light.

Some cars have mechanical brake wear sensors. These consist of a thin piece metal that will scrape on your brake rotors when the pads become too thin. However, they are not always reliable.

When you apply the brakes, they should feel firm and not make any noise. Once you start to hear your brakes squeaking or grinding, that can be signs of trouble.

If the brake pedal feels too soft or slowly sinks to the floor, then you need to get the car into the repair shop right away.

If you apply the brakes and the car pulls to the left or the right, this is another sign of brake trouble.

Most shops recommend brake pad replacement when the brakes get between 3-4 mm thick. When you get your brakes replaced, the shop will measure the thickness of the rotors. If they rotors are thick enough the brake rotors may be resurfaced. This is a process to make the brake rotor smooth, so the new brake pads have a clean rotor surface.

Some cars need new brake rotors at every brake replacement. Look into the manufacturer recommendations for your specific car.

The shop may also need to flush the brake system and replace with new fluid at that time.

## Flat Tire

Flat tires can happen at any place and at any time. We have seen many tires come in with low pressure due to nails or screws getting stuck in the tire tread. Most of these tires can be patched. Tires cannot be patched if the damage to the tire is on the sidewall or if the tire tread is too worn out. In these cases, the tire will need to be replaced.

Every driver should learn how to change a tire. You may never need to change your own tire, but at least you will know how to.

Yes, you can call for help to change your tire. Most of the time help will arrive quickly and you can be back on the road.

Some cars come with run-flat tires. This means that the car can lose air pressure, but you can still drive for some miles to get to the tire store.

Once you have a flat tire replaced with your spare, it's a good idea to head right over to the tire store and have them patch your tire. They will put the tire back on the car for you and put the spare tire back where it needs to go.

Sometimes the tire cannot be patched, and you will need to get a new tire. Most tire stores will sell you a set of two tires. This is a good idea if your other tire has little tread wear left.

As a general rule, it may be necessary to replace two tires. It may be a good idea to have two of the same tires on the front or rear of the car. Tires have different tread patterns and having similar tires will make the ride smoother. Check with the tire store to discuss this.

## Running Out of Gas

My daughter and her boyfriend were driving down to San Diego from Los Angeles. The fuel level function was not working on the car when they had to pull over (7 miles from my home) because they ran out of gas. There they were stuck on the side of the highway. Of course, my daughter called me for help.

But, luckily for them there is a truck that drives the highways looking for stranded motorists, drove by within five minutes of them pulling over.

The driver stopped and gave them some free gas. This was enough to get them to the gas station and then home to visit me. Most people aren't so fortunate to get help that quickly.

Running out of gas is a pain. It's loss of time and getting stuck is not fun at all.

Too many people wait until the last moment to fuel up. We all have busy schedules and drive from one place to the next without really planning our days.

Make it a point to fill up your gas tank when your fuel gauge gets to the 1/4 level.

Being prepared means not running out of gas.

Want to know more? Check out these FREE resources:

http://theautogirl.com/auto-care-for-women-downloads

# Chapter Ten
## What Buying a Shop has Taught Me

*I believe that people make their own luck by great preparation and good strategy.*
*~ Jack Canfield*

Just to confess, before I bought my business, I knew nothing about car repair. My kids called with car trouble and I dreaded the big car repair bill because I didn't understand what the shop was telling me.

I now know maintenance costs less than repairs, and if you neglect your car, repairs often cost more.

I've also learned you should find a shop you can trust and take your car to the same shop for almost everything.

If you think you're saving money by going to a quick-lube shop when and wherever it's convenient, you're missing the opportunity to have your car checked over for safety and other issues.

You also won't have the benefit of one place keeping records of all your car maintenance. This benefit alone can save you money in the long run by not duplicating services you've forgotten about.

In the time I've owned my shop, I've also learned a great deal from my customers. By listening to their complaints and concerns, I've learned how to better serve their needs.

## What Women Tell Me

I hear many women complaining about their auto repair service experiences. Sure, I hear complaints from men as well, however it is the women by far that don't feel they are treated fairly when taking their car in for service. They are intimidated, because they just don't know, and feel they have been taken advantage of when it comes to car repairs.

Buying a shop has taught me that there is a need for this book. So many people don't know enough about taking care of their car.

Take care of your car and it will take care of you!

## 10 Ways to Save Tons of Money

1.  Change the oil at 5,000 or 7,500 mileage intervals.

2.  Maintaining your car regularly can save you from costly breakdowns.

3.  Keep oil and coolant levels full to prevent engine damage.

4.  Check tire pressures regularly.

5.  Get a Pre-Purchase Inspection (PPI) before buying a used car.

6.  Keeping maintenance records.

7.  Service your transmission on a regular basis.

8.  Plan your road trip and check over the car first.

9.  Know what questions to ask at the auto repair shop.

10. Use what you've learned to Buy a good used car.

May the open road always take you where you want to go.

*Deborah Glazer-Wright*


Thank you for taking the time to read this book. Let me know how it goes at your next oil change!

I'd love you hear your comments, questions or ideas that you would like to share with me:

email: debbie@theautogirl.com

# Connect with Debbie Wright

**Blog:**
http://www.theAutoGirl.com

**LinkedIn:**
https://www.linkedin.com/in/deborahgwright/

**Facebook:**
https://www.facebook.com/TheAutoGirl/

**Instagram:**
https://www.instagram.com/the_auto_girl/

**Twitter:**
https://twitter.com/theautogirl

**Pinterest:**
https://www.pinterest.com/TheAutoGirl/

**YouTube:**
coming soon... The Auto Girl

**Amazon Author Page:**
http://www.Amazon.com/author/deborahglazerwright

# Other Books By
# Deborah J. Glazer-Wright

**The Auto Girl's Ultimate Guide for New Drivers (coming soon)**

## Please Leave Me a Review

If you found this book helpful, I would be very grateful if you would leave a review on Amazon.

Your comments really do make a difference. I read all reviews and listen to the feedback I receive. I'm always looking for ways to make this book even better.

Want to know more? Check out these FREE resources:

http://theautogirl.com/auto-care-for-women-downloads

www.ingramcontent.com/pod-product-compliance
Lightning Source LLC
Chambersburg PA
CBHW051758250726
48659CB00001B/488